US Citizenship Test Study Guide 2022 and 2023

Citizenship Test Book 2022 - 2023 for all 100
USCIS Civics Naturalization Exam Questions
[Includes Detailed Answer Explanations]

Anne Morris

Table of Contents

Introduction to the Citizenship Exam

General Information

The civics test is an oral exam taken as part of the process to become a U.S. citizen. You will be asked 10 questions and you must answer six of those questions correctly.

The 10 questions come from a list of 100 possible questions. All 100 questions and their answers are included in this guide for you to study.

Read the questions carefully because in some cases you will need to know more than one answer. For example:

> **9. What are <u>two</u> rights in the Declaration of Independence?**
>
> - Life
> - Liberty
> - Pursuit of happiness

This question is asking you to answer with two of the three options listed. Your answer is not correct if it only includes one option. For example, "life and pursuit of happiness" is a correct answer to the question, but "pursuit of happiness" alone is incorrect.

Changing Questions

Some of the answers to the questions can change, such as the name of the U.S. President or the Speaker of the House. Other answers depend on where you live, such as the name of your governor. For these questions, please check out our website where we provide up-to-date answers:

testprepbooks.com/civics

Seniors

If you are 65 years old or older and have been a legal permanent resident of the United States for 20 or more years, you may study just the questions that have been marked with an asterisk*.

Feedback

We are honored to be a part of your success journey. If you have any questions about this book, please email us at:

info@studyguideteam.com

American Government

Principles of American Democracy

1. What is the supreme law of the land?

- The Constitution

The Constitution was established in 1789 as the ruling document of the United States of America.

2. What does the Constitution do?

- Sets up the government
- Defines the government
- Protects the basic rights of Americans

The Constitution outlines the branches of the United States government and defines the role of each branch. It also states the rights that Americans have and balances power between the state governments and the federal (national) government in Washington, D.C.

3. The idea of self-government is in the first three words of the Constitution. What are these words?

- We the People

The Constitution begins with the words "We the People" to emphasize that the U.S. government was created by its citizens for the benefit of the people.

4. What is an amendment?

- A change to the Constitution
- An addition to the Constitution

An amendment is an addition to the Constitution that either changes a current portion of the Constitution or adds a new portion. The Constitution has been amended 27 times.

5. What do we call the first ten amendments to the Constitution?

- The Bill of Rights

The first 10 amendments are called the Bill of Rights because they outline specific rights for Americans. These rights include things like freedom of speech, the right to an attorney, and the right to a trial.

6. What is <u>one</u> right or freedom from the First Amendment?*

- Speech
- Religion
- Assembly
- Press
- Petition the government

The first amendment is in the Bill of Rights. It states that the government is not allowed to restrict or prohibit people's speech, religion, right to assemble, the right to express ideas and beliefs publicly, or the right to petition the government for change.

7. How many amendments does the Constitution have?

- Twenty-seven (27)

The U.S. Constitution was drafted and signed in 1787. In 1789 there were 12 amendments proposed to change the constitution. 10 of these amendments, later known as the Bill of Rights, were added to the Constitution. Since then, 17 more amendments have been added to the Constitution.

8. What did the Declaration of Independence do?

- Announced our independence from Great Britain
- Declared our independence from Great Britain
- Stated that the United States is free from Great Britain

The United States fought the Revolutionary War against Great Britain in order to gain their independence. The Declaration of Independence was drafted and signed in 1776, 1 year after the war began and 7 years before the war ended. The Declaration of Independence, as its name suggests, declared the independence of the United States from British control.

9. What are <u>two</u> rights in the Declaration of Independence?

- Life
- Liberty
- Pursuit of happiness

The Declaration of Independence begins its second paragraph with the statement, "We hold these truths to be self-evident, that all men are created equal, that they are endowed by their Creator with certain unalienable Rights, that among these are **Life, Liberty** and the **pursuit of Happiness.**"

10. What is freedom of religion?

- You can practice any religion, or not practice a religion.

Many people who came to the United States from Europe were fleeing religious persecution. Freedom of religion is the ability to practice whatever religion that an individual would like to, or no religion at all, without negative consequences from the government.

11. What is the economic system in the United States?*

- Capitalist economy
- Market economy

A capitalist economy or a market economy is one where the people of a country own their own private property and goods and engage in the free and open trade of such things.

12. What is the "rule of law"?

- Everyone must follow the law.
- Leaders must obey the law.
- Government must obey the law.
- No one is above the law.

The rule of law was established to make sure that every individual is held accountable to all the laws that the people agree upon. This includes those in authority as well; no person should be above the law.

System of Government

13. Name <u>one</u> branch or part of the government.*

- Congress
- Legislative
- President
- Executive
- The courts
- Judicial

The United States government was created with 3 branches, or parts. Each branch consists of a primary person or group of people who operate or make up the specific branch. The Legislative branch creates the laws (Congress is the legislative branch). The Executive branch carries out the laws (the President runs the

Executive branch). Finally, the Judicial branch evaluates and interprets the laws (the courts are the Judicial branch).

14. What stops <u>one</u> branch of government from becoming too powerful?

- Checks and balances
- Separation of powers

The purpose of dividing the government into 3 branches was to divide the three different powers of government (legislative, executive, and judicial) between different people or groups of people to limit the power any individual person or group can have over the United States. This is called the separation of powers. The system of checks and balances means that each branch has the authority to check, or stop, certain actions by the other two branches, which keeps control and power balanced between many people to make sure no one takes too much authority.

15. Who is in charge of the executive branch?

- The President

The President has the responsibility of accepting or rejecting the bills proposed by Congress based on the best interest of the people of the United States, whom he/she has been elected to represent. If the President accepts and signs a bill, it becomes a law. The President is also responsible for executing, or enforcing, the laws of the United States.

16. Who makes federal laws?

- Congress
- Senate and House of Representatives
- U.S. or national legislature

Congress creates the laws that govern the United States, but Congress cannot pass a law without the President's approval. However, if the President rejects or vetoes a law, Congress can still pass the law by overturning the veto with a two-thirds (2/3) majority vote.

17. What are the <u>two</u> parts of the U.S. Congress?*

- The Senate and the House of Representatives

Congress is divided up into 2 houses, or chambers: the House of Representatives and the Senate. Each chamber is made up of elected officials who create laws for the United States. Each state is represented equally in the Senate (2 per state) and proportionally in the House based on population.

18. How many U.S. Senators are there?

- One hundred (100)

There are 2 Senators for each state for a total of 100 Senators. Senators, along with members of the House of Representatives, draft, amend, and vote on federal legislation that governs U.S. domestic and foreign policy. Senators confirm or reject executive nominations and treaties and act as the court for trying impeachment cases to hold all federal officers accountable to the law.

19. We elect a U.S. Senator for how many years?

- Six (6)

Senators serve for 6-year terms. This helps ensure that the Senators that are in office are still truly representing the people of their state while also looking out for the long-term interests of the United States as a whole. After 6 years the Senators can run for office again. There are no limits on the number of years a Senator can hold office.

20. Who is <u>one</u> of your state's U.S. Senators now?*

- Answers will vary according to your state. You can find your U.S. Senators here:

testprepbooks.com/civics

Every state has 2 Senators that represent the people of that state.

District of Columbia residents and residents of U.S. territories should answer that D.C. (or the territory where the applicant lives) has no U.S. Senators.

21. The House of Representatives has how many voting members?

- Four hundred thirty-five (435)

The House of Representatives is made up of elected officials from every state. The number of Representatives from each state is determined based on the number of citizens living in the state. There is 1 Representative for every 30,000 citizens and each state is required to have at least 1 Representative. Representatives, along with Senators, draft, amend, and vote on federal legislation. Revenue bills and impeachment must both start in the House of Representatives, although impeachments are tried in the Senate.

22. We elect a U.S. Representative for how many years?

- Two (2)

U.S. Representatives are elected every 2 years. This helps ensure that the Representatives that are in office are still truly representing the people of their state without having such frequent turnover that nothing gets done. After 2 years the Representatives can run for office again. There are no limits on the number of years a Representative can hold office.

23. Name your U.S. Representative.

- Answers will vary. You can find your U.S. Representative here:

testprepbooks.com/civics

Every state has at least 1 U.S. Representative.

Residents of territories with nonvoting Delegates or Resident Commissioners may provide the name of the Delegate or Commissioner. Also acceptable is any statement that the territory has no (voting) Representatives in Congress.

24. Who does a U.S. Senator represent?

- All people of the state

A U.S. Senator represents everybody in the state where he/she was elected.

25. Why do some states have more Representatives than other states?

- (because of) the state's population
- (because) they have more people
- (because) some states have more people

Each state is allowed 1 Representative in the House of Representatives for every 30,000 citizens, and each state must have at least 1 Representative. This is different from the Senate, where every state has 2 Senators no matter how many citizens they have.

26. We elect a President for how many years?

- Four (4)

Presidents are elected for 4-year terms and are only allowed to serve 2 terms for a total of 8 years in office.

27. In what month do we vote for President?*

- November

The President is elected in November and sworn into office on January 6th of the following year.

28. What is the name of the President of the United States now?*

- Joseph R. Biden, Jr.
- Joe Biden
- Biden

In 2020, former Vice President Joseph Biden was elected as the President of the United States of America.

The answer to this question can change. Access this website for up-to-date information:

testprepbooks.com/civics

29. What is the name of the Vice President of the United States now?

- Kamala D. Harris
- Kamala Harris
- Harris

President Joseph Biden selected Kamala Harris to be his Vice President in 2020.

The answer to this question can change. Access this website for up-to-date information:

testprepbooks.com/civics

30. If the President can no longer serve, who becomes President?

- The Vice President

If the President dies or has become unfit for office, the Vice President will then act as President.

31. If both the President and the Vice President can no longer serve, who becomes President?

- The Speaker of the House

If both the President and the Vice President die or have become unfit for office, the Speaker of the House will then act as President. The Speaker of the House is elected by the Representatives in the House of Representatives and is the leader of the House of Representatives.

32. Who is the Commander in Chief of the military?

- The President

The President is the highest military authority in the United States and is responsible for maintaining the military and commissioning military officers. However, Congress is responsible for funding the military and Congress is the only branch of government that can declare war.

33. Who signs bills to become laws?

- The President

Since the president is in charge of the Executive branch, he/she is tasked with signing bills into laws. Congress drafts bills and then sends them to the President, who must sign the bill to create a new law.

34. Who vetoes bills?

- The President

The President has the right to veto or reject any bills that Congress sends to him/her to be made into laws. Congress can overturn the President's veto with a two-thirds (2/3) majority vote.

35. What does the President's Cabinet do?

- Advises the President

Members of the President's Cabinet are selected by the President to serve as his/her advisory staff. Each Cabinet member is in charge of a different part of the Executive branch, called executive departments. Some examples are the Department of the Treasury, the Department of Defense, and the Department of Education. The cabinet members are referred to as the Secretary of their department. The Vice President is also a member of the President's Cabinet.

36. What are <u>two</u> Cabinet-level positions?

- Secretary of Agriculture
- Secretary of Commerce
- Secretary of Defense
- Secretary of Education
- Secretary of Energy
- Secretary of Health and Human Services
- Secretary of Homeland Security
- Secretary of Housing and Urban Development
- Secretary of the Interior
- Secretary of Labor
- Secretary of State
- Secretary of Transportation
- Secretary of the Treasury

- Secretary of Veterans Affairs
- Attorney General
- Vice President

There are 16 members of the Presidential Cabinet. Each member advises the President concerning the executive department he/she is in charge of.

37. What does the judicial branch do?

- Reviews laws
- Explains laws
- Resolves disputes (disagreements)
- Decides if a law goes against the Constitution

The Judicial branch is tasked with interpreting laws and judging if they agree with the Constitution. The Constitution is the highest law of the land and overrules any other laws that disagree with it.

38. What is the highest court in the United States?

- The Supreme Court

There are local and state courts that handle various levels of smaller claims and issues. The first level of federal (national) courts are the District Courts. The second level of federal courts are the Courts of Appeals. The highest court in the United States is the Supreme Court.

39. How many justices are on the Supreme Court?

- Nine (9)

Since the judicial branch is tasked with evaluating laws, there are an odd number of Supreme Court Justices to make sure that a vote on any decision is not tied.

The answer to this question can change. Access this website for up-to-date information:

testprepbooks.com/civics

40. Who is the Chief Justice of the United States now?

- John Roberts (John G. Roberts, Jr.)

The Chief Justice is the one who leads the other justices in their discussions and he/she is greatly influential in choosing what cases are heard by the court. However, the Chief Justice's vote counts the same as the other justices.

The answer to this question can change. Access this website for up-to-date information:

testprepbooks.com/civics

41. Under our Constitution, some powers belong to the federal government. What is <u>one</u> power of the federal government?

- To print money
- To declare war
- To create an army
- To make treaties

The Constitution of the United States gave the federal (national) government the powers it needed in order to manage the affairs of the United States and maintain its sovereignty. The powers given specifically to the federal government are called delegated powers.

42. Under our Constitution, some powers belong to the states. What is <u>one</u> power of the states?

- Provide schooling and education
- Provide protection (police)
- Provide safety (fire departments)
- Give a driver's license
- Approve zoning and land use

The Constitution divided powers between the federal government and the states to prevent the federal government from becoming too powerful. Certain powers were given only to the federal government, while all other powers belonged to the states. The powers given to the federal government are called delegated powers and those belonging to the states are called reserved powers.

43. Who is the Governor of your state now?

- Answers will vary

You can find your Governor here:

testprepbooks.com/civics

State Governors are elected by the people of their state or territory to serve as the state or territory's chief executive officer. The Governors are responsible for executing the laws for their states and running their state's executive branch, just like the President does for the U.S. as a whole. Specific powers for each governor are laid out in the state or territory's Constitution.

District of Columbia residents should answer that D.C. does not have a Governor.

44. What is the capital of your state?*

- Answers will vary.

You can find your state capital here:

testprepbooks.com/civics

The state capital is the city where the legislative branch of the state's government meets and where the major government offices are located.

District of Columbia residents should answer that D.C. is not a state and does not have a capital. Residents of U.S. territories should name the capital of the territory.

45. What are the <u>two</u> major political parties in the United States?*

- Democratic and Republican

There are two primary political parties in the United States, the Democratic Party and the Republican Party. While no one is required to participate in either party, and there are other political parties that are much smaller, government officials are usually from either the Republican Party or the Democratic Party.

46. What is the political party of the President now?

- Democratic (party)

Joseph Biden is part of the Democratic party.

The answer to this question can change. Access this website for up-to-date information:

testprepbooks.com/civics

47. What is the name of the Speaker of the House of Representatives now?

- Nancy P. Pelosi
- Nancy Pelosi
- Pelosi

Nancy Pelosi, a member of the Democratic Party, was elected to be the Speaker of the House. The Speaker of the House is the leader of the House of Representatives and has control over what issues are discussed when the House of Representatives meets.

Rights and Responsibilities

48. There are four amendments to the Constitution about who can vote. Describe <u>one</u> of them.

- Citizens eighteen (18) and older (can vote).
- You don't have to pay (a poll tax) to vote.
- Any citizen can vote. (Women and men can vote.)
- A male citizen of any race (can vote).

When the Constitution was created in 1776, only white men who were 21 and older and owned land could vote. Over the next two centuries the list of eligible voters grew to include all men and women of any race regardless of land ownership, and the voting age was lowered from 21 years old to 18 years old.

49. What is <u>one</u> responsibility that is only for United States citizens?*

- Serve on a jury
- Vote in a federal election

There are many benefits and rights that only pertain to the citizens of the United States. In order to preserve those rights and benefits, every citizen also has certain responsibilities to serve their country. Voting in a federal election is both a right and a responsibility; citizens have the right to choose who will rule them and have the duty to choose wisely. Serving on a jury means being part of a trial or series of trials in a court. It is a way for citizens to make sure that the people of the United States receive justice in the courts.

50. Name <u>one</u> right only for United States citizens.

- Vote in a federal election
- Run for federal office

There are many rights enjoyed only by citizens of the United States. Some of those are the right to vote in an election, run for office, freely leave and reenter the country, etc.

51. What are <u>two</u> rights of everyone living in the United States?

- Freedom of expression
- Freedom of speech
- Freedom of assembly
- Freedom to petition the government
- Freedom of religion
- The right to bear arms

While non-citizens of the United States do not have certain rights that are specifically limited to citizens, there are many rights that belong to anyone living in the United States. The first amendment rights of free exercise of religion, freedom of speech and the press, freedom of assembly, and freedom to petition the government apply to everyone. The second amendment right to keep and bear arms is also applied to everyone living in the United States; however, there are some restrictions on this right.

52. What do we show loyalty to when we say the Pledge of Allegiance?

- The United States
- The flag

The Pledge of Allegiance states: "I pledge allegiance to the Flag of the United States of America and to the Republic for which it stands, one nation under God, indivisible, with liberty and justice for all."

53. What is <u>one</u> promise you make when you become a United States citizen?

- Give up loyalty to other countries
- Defend the Constitution and laws of the United States
- Obey the laws of the United States
- Serve in the U.S. military (if needed)
- Serve (do important work for) the nation (if needed)
- Be loyal to the United States

The Oath of Allegiance, sworn as the last step in becoming a U.S. citizen, states:

"I hereby declare, on oath, that I absolutely and entirely renounce and abjure all allegiance and fidelity to any foreign prince, potentate, state, or sovereignty, of whom or which I have heretofore been a subject or citizen;

...that I will support and defend the Constitution and laws of the United States of America against all enemies, foreign and domestic;

...that I will bear true faith and allegiance to the same;

...that I will bear arms on behalf of the United States when required by the law;

...that I will perform noncombatant service in the Armed Forces of the United States when required by the law;

...that I will perform work of national importance under civilian direction when required by the law; and

...that I take this obligation freely, without any mental reservation or purpose of evasion; so help me God."

54. How old do citizens have to be to vote for President?*

- Eighteen (18) and older

The 26th Amendment to the Constitution lowered the voting age from 21 years old to 18 years old. Every U.S. citizen 18 years and older has the right to vote, with a few specific restrictions. Some states have voting restrictions on people who are mentally incapacitated or who have felonies, and U.S. citizens living in U.S. territories can't vote for the President in the general election.

55. What are <u>two</u> ways that Americans can participate in their democracy?

- Vote
- Join a political party
- Help with a campaign
- Join a civic group
- Join a community group
- Give an elected official your opinion on an issue
- Call Senators and Representatives
- Publicly support or oppose an issue or policy
- Run for office
- Write to a newspaper

America encourages participation in the government. The Constitution states that the government is "by the people, for the people." In order to keep America "by the people," the people must be involved in the governance of the nation. There are many ways to get involved that range from voting in elections to running for office yourself. The only offices naturalized citizens can't hold are President and Vice President.

56. When is the last day you can send in federal income tax forms?*

- April 15

Federal income tax is a tax that is paid to fund the federal government from the wages people earn from their work. Every citizen is required to file taxes for their own income each year.

57. When must all men register for the Selective Service?

- At age eighteen (18)
- Between eighteen (18) and twenty-six (26)

All male citizens are required to sign up for Selective Service within 30 days of their 18th birthday, although late registrations are accepted until a male citizen's 26th birthday. Failure to sign up is a federal offense. Selective Service is the United States military draft. If the U.S. is fighting a war, it can draft men signed up for the Selective Service to go and serve in the military. The last draft was in 1973.

American History

Colonial Period and Independence

58. What is <u>one</u> reason colonists came to America?

- Freedom
- Political liberty
- Religious freedom
- Economic opportunity
- Practice their religion
- Escape persecution

The first European colony in the United States was founded in 1607 at Jamestown, Virginia. Colonists came to the United States from all over Europe seeking religious freedom and new economic opportunities.

59. Who lived in America before the Europeans arrived?

- American Indians
- Native Americans

Before Europeans came to America, there were already people living here. Those people were Native Americans (or American Indians). While they were less technologically developed than the Europeans, the Native American tribes had rich cultures and economies based on hunting, agriculture, and war.

60. What group of people was taken to America and sold as slaves?

- Africans
- People from Africa

Africans were sold in Africa by their own people or taken as prisoners of war by other tribes and sent throughout the world as slaves. In 1619, slaves captured from a Portuguese ship were brought to Jamestown, the first U.S. colonist site, although slavery existed in other portions of the U.S., Central America, and South America much earlier than that. Africans and people of African descent were legally used as slave labor in the U.S. until the 13th Amendment was added to the Constitution in 1865.

61. Why did the colonists fight the British?

- Because of high taxes (taxation without representation)
- Because the British army stayed in their houses (boarding, quartering)
- Because they didn't have self-government

The colonists fought against the British because they were unable to live in freedom. They were British citizens before the Revolutionary War, but they were taxed without being represented in the British government, they were forced to let British soldiers stay in their homes, and they were ruled by British officials rather than people they elected themselves. All of these injustices led them to revolt against British rule and create their own independent country, the United States of America.

62. Who wrote the Declaration of Independence?

• Thomas Jefferson

The Declaration of Independence was written in 1776 by Thomas Jefferson, a lawyer from Virginia. The main goal of the Declaration was to explain why the United States was declaring independence from Great Britain. It laid out the basic political theory that has defined the United States: "We hold these truths to be self-evident, that all men are created equal, that they are endowed by their Creator with certain unalienable Rights, that among these are Life, Liberty and the pursuit of Happiness.—That to secure these rights,

Governments are instituted among Men, deriving their just powers from the consent of the governed...."

63. When was the Declaration of Independence adopted?

- July 4, 1776

While the Declaration of Independence was adopted on July 4, 1776, the fifty-six men who signed it did not begin doing so until August 2, 1776. Once signed, the document officially declared the United States as independent from Great Britain. The men who signed the declaration held many different occupations, including lawyers, merchants, doctors, plantation owners, and ministers. The United States finally won freedom from Great Britain when the Revolutionary War ended seven years later.

64. There were 13 original states. Name three.

- New Hampshire
- Massachusetts
- Rhode Island
- Connecticut
- New York
- New Jersey
- Pennsylvania
- Delaware

- Maryland
- Virginia
- North Carolina
- South Carolina
- Georgia

The original 13 states were located on the East Coast of the United States. Before they became states, they were colonies of Great Britain.

65. What happened at the Constitutional Convention?

- The Constitution was written
- The Founding Fathers wrote the Constitution

The Constitutional Convention met in Philadelphia in May 1787. Its goal was to create a stronger federal government after a series of economic troubles and a rebellion made it clear that the Articles of Confederation, the first attempt at governing the United States, were not working. Eventually, delegates at the Convention realized that changing the Articles of Confederation would not be enough and they decided to write the Constitution instead and create an entirely new system of government.

66. When was the Constitution written?

- 1787

Delegates from every state except Rhode Island met in Philadelphia in May 1787 to change the government that was put in place under the Articles of Confederation. However, they soon realized that they needed to start over and create an entirely new system of government for the United States. On September 17, 1787, 39 of the 55 delegates signed the Constitution and it was presented to the people of the United States for ratification.

67. The Federalist Papers supported the passage of the U.S. Constitution. Name one of the writers.

- James Madison
- Alexander Hamilton
- John Jay
- Publius

The Federalist Papers were a series of articles published in New York newspapers in 1787 and 1788 that encouraged voters to ratify the new Constitution of the United States and get rid of the Articles of Confederation. They were written anonymously under the pen name Publius, but in the 1800s it became public knowledge that Alexander Hamilton, James Madison, and John Jay were the authors. The essays give detailed explanations of different parts of the Constitution and outline the reasons why adopting the Constitution would benefit the United States.

68. What is <u>one</u> thing Benjamin Franklin is famous for?

- U.S. diplomat
- Oldest member of the Constitutional Convention
- First Postmaster General of the United States
- Writer of "Poor Richard's Almanac"
- Started the first free libraries

Benjamin Franklin was an eccentric and intelligent man known for many things. He was an inventor, a U.S. diplomat to France during the Revolutionary War, and the first Postmaster General of the U.S. As a writer, he is known for his autobiography and *Poor Richard's Almanac*. He was the oldest delegate at the Constitutional Convention. Franklin was also the only person to sign all four documents that laid the foundation for the United States: The Declaration of Independence (1776), the Treaty of Alliance with France (1778), the Treaty of Paris (1783) that ended the Revolutionary War, and the Constitution (1787).

69. Who is the "Father of Our Country"?

- George Washington

George Washington is one of the greatest figures in American history. As the commander of the Continental Army, he led the United States to victory against Great Britain in the Revolutionary War. He was unanimously elected as the first President of the United States, and his actions and speeches while in office set guidelines that Presidents still follow today.

70. Who was the first President?*

- George Washington

On April 30, 1789, George Washington gave his first speech as the first President of the United States. This speech is now known as the first Presidential Inaugural Address and has served as a pattern for Presidents ever since.

1800s

71. What territory did the United States buy from France in 1803?

- The Louisiana Territory
- Louisiana

President Thomas Jefferson purchased The Louisiana Territory from France in 1803. It was composed of 530,000,000 acres and double the size of the United States. The land area went from the Rocky Mountains to the Mississippi River. It also went up from present-day Louisiana all the way to Canada. In addition, it made sure the U.S. had access to the port of New Orleans and the Mississippi River for shipping materials and supplies to western settlements.

72. Name <u>one</u> war fought by the United States in the 1800s.

- War of 1812
- Mexican-American War
- Civil War
- Spanish-American War

The War of 1812: as part of the Napoleonic Wars between France and Great Britain, Great Britain tried to prevent the U.S. from trading with France, impressed (or forced) American seamen to serve on British ships, and supported Native American tribes who tried to stop U.S. westward expansion. Many in the U.S. considered the War of 1812 a second war of independence because the U.S. fought off the British, Canadian, and Native American forces and preserved their independence.

The Mexican-American War: when the U.S. made Texas part of the country in 1845, there was a fight over the location of the border between Texas and Mexico. President James Polk declared war against Mexico in 1846 and the U.S. invaded Mexico City, the Mexican capital, in 1847. The treaty ending the war sold territory that became New Mexico, Utah, Nevada, Arizona, California, Texas, and part of Colorado to the U.S for $15 million.

Civil War: the Civil War was fought between two sections of the U.S. over a number of issues. The main issues were economic concerns, states' vs. federal rights, and slavery. The Northern states (the Union, anti-slavery) fought against the Southern states (the Confederates, pro-slavery). The war began in 1861 and ended in 1865. The Union defeated the

Confederates, ended slavery, and kept the U.S. together as one nation.

Spanish-American War: in April 1898, the U.S. chose to aid Cuba in its fight for independence and declared war on Spain. The war lasted until December of the same year and resulted in Cuba's independence and the U.S. acquiring Guam, Puerto Rico, and the Philippines.

73. Name the U.S. war between the North and the South.

- The Civil War
- The War between the States

The Northern states, known as the Union, fought against the Southern States, known as the Confederates. The main issues of the war were economic concerns, states' vs. federal rights, and slavery. The war began in 1861 and ended in 1865. The Union defeated the Confederates, ended slavery, and kept the U.S. together as one nation.

74. Name <u>one</u> problem that led to the Civil War.

- Slavery
- Economic reasons
- States' rights

The main issues of the Civil War were economic concerns, states' vs. federal rights, and slavery. The Northern states (the Union, anti-slavery) fought against the Southern states (the Confederates, pro-slavery). The war began in 1861 and ended in 1865. The Union defeated the Confederates, abolished slavery, and kept the U.S. together as one nation.

75. What was <u>one</u> important thing that Abraham Lincoln did?*

- Freed the slaves (Emancipation Proclamation)
- Saved (or preserved) the Union
- Led the United States during the Civil War

Abraham Lincoln, the 16th president of the U.S., led the U.S. during the Civil War (1861-1865). He was a brilliant politician, and his speeches are still used to explain and understand the relationships between the Constitution, the states, and the people of the U.S. The generals he appointed defeated the Confederate states, and he freed all slaves in the Confederate states with his Emancipation Proclamation. One of the most important things he did was save the Union – he made sure that the United States stayed one, united nation.

76. What did the Emancipation Proclamation do?

- Freed the slaves
- Freed slaves in the Confederacy
- Freed slaves in the Confederate states
- Freed slaves in most Southern states

The Emancipation Proclamation was a speech by President Abraham Lincoln in 1863. This proclamation freed all slaves in the Confederate (Southern) states, although many Southern slaves were unaware of their freedom since their slave owners did not release them. The slaves were freed as the Union (Northern) army captured more and more of the Confederate states in the Civil War, and all slaves in the U.S. were freed in 1865 when the 13th Amendment was added to the Constitution.

77. What did Susan B. Anthony do?

- Fought for women's rights
- Fought for civil rights

Susan B. Anthony (1820-1906) fought for the rights of women and slaves. She was an abolitionist during the Civil War who fought to end slavery. Both before and after the war, she fought for woman to have the right to vote, and her work eventually helped lead to the

19th Amendment being added to the U.S. Constitution.

Recent American History and Other Important Historical Information

78. Name <u>one</u> war fought by the United States in the 1900s.*

- World War I
- World War II
- Korean War
- Vietnam War
- (Persian) Gulf War

World War I: this war began in Austria in 1914 and quickly turned into a worldwide conflict. The two sides were the Central Powers (Germany, Austria-Hungary, and Turkey) and the Allies (France, Great Britain, Russia, Italy, Japan, and the U.S. after 1917). America stayed neutral until 1917, and then joined the war for two reasons. The first reason was that Germany decided to use its submarines to sink any ships in the waters near Great Britain, even if they were American ships that were neutral in the war. This was called unrestricted submarine warfare. The second reason was that Germany tried to get Mexico to support them by promising to help Mexico take back the land they lost to the U.S. in the Mexican-American War.

This information was in the Zimmerman Telegram. The war lasted until 1918 when Germany surrendered to the Allied forces.

World War II: this war began in 1939 when Germany invaded Poland. Like World War I, it quickly turned into a worldwide conflict. The two sides were the Axis powers (Germany, Italy, and Japan) and the Allies (France, Great Britain, and Soviet Union, and the United States after 1941). The U.S. remained neutral until 1941 when Japan bombed Pearl Harbor, a U.S. military base in Hawaii. The war ended in 1945 with the defeat of Nazi Germany.

Korean War: this war began as a civil war between North Korea and South Korea. It was the first armed conflict of the Cold War, a long period of political and military rivalry between the Soviet Union and the United States and their allies. The war began in 1950 and ended in 1953 with an armistice that ended the fighting. No peace treaty was signed; however, in 2021, South Korea announced that they have a possible draft of peace treaty.

Vietnam War: this war, much like the Korean War, was part of the Cold War and was fought to stop the spread of Communism. It was also a civil war, with Communist North Vietnam fighting South Vietnam, which was supported first by the French and then by the U.S. The U.S. became involved in 1954 after the French left. In 1964, Congress gave President Lyndon B. Johnson permission to use a huge amount of force against the Northern Vietnamese. The war was very unpopular in the U.S., and the U.S. withdrew their troops in 1973. The war ended with the defeat of South Vietnam in 1975.

(Persian) Gulf War: this war only lasted 43 days. It started when Iraq invaded its neighboring county, Kuwait. The United Nations and others immediately condemned Iraq. The U.S. and Great Britain sent troops to the area and called for other nations to do the same. The U.S.-led coalition, the largest since World War II, responded with a two-part offensive known as Operation Desert Storm. It started with a relentless 42 day air attack and ended with a 100 hour ground assault that liberated Kuwait.

79. Who was President during World War I?

- Woodrow Wilson

Woodrow Wilson served from 1913 – 1921.

80. Who was the President during the Great Depression and World War II?

- Franklin Roosevelt

The Great Depression lasted from 1929 to about 1939. It was caused by a number of economic failures, most particularly the crash of the New York Stock Exchange on October 24, 1929, that left the country with record high levels of unemployment. It was the worst economic crisis in the history of the U.S.

81. Who did the United States fight in World War II?

- Japan, Germany, and Italy

Japan, Germany, and Italy made up the Axis powers. The Allied powers were France, Great Britain, the U.S., and the Soviet Union.

82. Before he was President, Eisenhower was a general. What war was he in?

- World War II

Eisenhower was the supreme commander of Allied forces in World War II. He was the one responsible for the successful 1944 invasion of France known as D-Day.

83. During the Cold War, what was the main concern of the United States?

- Communism

The Cold War was a long period of political and military rivalry between the Soviet Union and the United States and their allies. The main concern for the U.S. was to stop the spread of Communism across the world.

84. What movement tried to end racial discrimination?

- Civil Rights Movement

Despite the fact that slavery legally ended in 1863 with the 13th Amendment to the Constitution, there were still many racially unequal practices in the U.S. The Civil Rights Movement (1954 – 1968), sought to gain equality for all people in America.

85. What did Martin Luther King Jr. do?*

- Fought for civil rights
- Worked for equality for all Americans

A key leader in the Civil Rights Movement was Martin Luther King, Jr. He peacefully led protests throughout the country and petitioned the government to grant rights to all people. He is well known for his speech, "I Have a Dream."

86. What major event happened on September 11, 2001, in the United States?

- Terrorists attacked the United States

On September 11, 2001 (9/11), terrorist forces known as al Qaeda crashed two planes into the Twin Towers of the World Trade Center in New York and one plane into the Pentagon in Arlington, VA. A fourth plane crashed in a field in Pennsylvania when the passengers fought the terrorists who hijacked the plane. There were roughly 3,000 deaths caused by these attacks; most of them were civilians. This attack triggered the War on Terror.

87. Name one American Indian tribe in the United States.

- Cherokee
- Navajo
- Sioux
- Chippewa
- Choctaw
- Pueblo
- Apache
- Iroquois

- Creek
- Blackfeet
- Seminole
- Cheyenne
- Arawak
- Shawnee
- Mohegan
- Huron
- Oneida
- Lakota
- Crow
- Teton
- Hopi
- Inuit

Since there are many other tribes in the United States, the USCIS Officers will be given a list of federally recognized American Indian tribes.

Before Europeans came to America, there were already people living here. Those people were Native Americans (or American Indians). While they were less technologically developed than the Europeans, the Native American tribes had rich cultures and economies based on hunting, agriculture, and war.

Integrated Civics

Geography

88. Name <u>one</u> of the two longest rivers in the United States.

- Missouri River
- Mississippi River

The Missouri River is 2,341 miles long. It begins in southwestern Montana; flows through Montana, North Dakota, Nebraska, Iowa, Kansas, and Missouri; and empties into the Mississippi River at St. Louis, Missouri.

The Mississippi River is 2,340 miles long. It begins in northern Minnesota; flows through Minnesota, Wisconsin, Iowa, Illinois, Missouri, Kentucky, Tennessee, Arkansas, Mississippi, and Louisiana; and empties in the Gulf of Mexico.

89. What ocean is on the West Coast of the United States?

- Pacific Ocean

There is one large world ocean that is divided into 5 parts: the Pacific Ocean, the Atlantic Ocean, the Indian

Ocean, the Southern Ocean, and the Arctic Ocean. Two of these oceans border the United States: the Pacific Ocean (which is the largest ocean) on the West Coast, and the Atlantic Ocean on the East Coast.

The states of California, Oregon, and Washington, all on the West Coast, border the Pacific Ocean.

90. What ocean is on the East Coast of the United States?

- Atlantic Ocean

There is one large world ocean that is divided into 5 parts: the Pacific Ocean, the Atlantic Ocean, the Indian Ocean, the Southern Ocean, and the Arctic Ocean. Two of these oceans border the United States: the Pacific Ocean (which is the largest ocean) on the West Coast, and the Atlantic Ocean on the East Coast.

On the East Coast, the states of Maine, New Hampshire, Massachusetts, Connecticut, Rhode Island, New York, New Jersey, Delaware, Maryland, Virginia, North Carolina, South Carolina, Georgia, and Florida all border the Atlantic Ocean.

91. Name <u>one</u> U.S. territory.

- Puerto Rico
- U.S. Virgin Islands

- American Samoa
- Northern Mariana Islands
- Guam

A U.S. Territory is a place that remains self-governed but is under the authority of the United States. Territories do not enjoy the same rights as states, although their people are U.S. citizens except in American Samoa.

92. Name <u>one</u> state that borders Canada.

- Maine
- New Hampshire
- Vermont
- New York
- Pennsylvania
- Ohio
- Michigan
- Minnesota
- North Dakota
- Montana
- Idaho
- Washington
- Alaska

Canada is the large country directly north of the U.S. They are allies with the U.S. and share 5,525 miles of border with 13 U.S. states.

93. Name <u>one</u> state that borders Mexico.

- California
- Arizona
- New Mexico
- Texas

Mexico is the country directly south of the U.S. It is smaller in size and shares 1,954 miles of border with 4 U.S. states.

94. What is the capital of the United States?*

- Washington, D.C.

The capital is where the three branches of the U.S. government meet. Washington, D.C., is not a state; it is a district between Maryland and Virginia. The Constitution made sure that the capital would be separate from any state. This was to make sure that no one state was more important than the others and to make sure that the capital city was not more loyal to one state than any others.

95. Where is the Statue of Liberty?*

- New York (Harbor)
- Liberty Island
- Also acceptable are New Jersey, near New York City, and on the Hudson River.

The Statue of Liberty was a gift of friendship to the U.S. from France in 1886. Now green with age, the copper statue was once shiny and bright. The statue symbolizes freedom and democracy and stands on Liberty Island in New York Harbor.

Symbols

96. Why does the flag have 13 stripes?

- Because there were 13 original colonies
- Because the stripes represent the original colonies

When the U.S. voted to officially declare its independence from Great Britain on July 2, 1776, there were 13 colonies on the East Coast. These colonies became the first 13 states. The flag represents those first states by having 13 red and white stripes. The union of the flag, or the blue part with white stars, has 1 star for every state in the U.S. (50 states).

97. Why does the flag have 50 stars?*

- Because there is one star for each state
- Because each star represents a state
- Because there are 50 states

The stars on the flag represent the 50 states in the U.S. The union of the flag, or the blue part with white stars, has 1 star for every current state in the U.S. The last state to be added was Hawaii in 1959.

98. What is the name of the national anthem?

- The Star-Spangled Banner

The "Star-Spangled Banner" was composed in 1814 by Francis Scott Key. He wrote the poem while he was aboard a British ship watching the British attack Fort McHenry in Baltimore during the War of 1812. Over 1,500 cannons were fired that night. In the morning, however, the American flag still flew over the fort.

Holidays

99. When do we celebrate Independence Day?*

- July 4

Independence Day celebrates the day the U.S. adopted the Declaration of Independence, a document officially declaring the U.S. independent from Great Britain. The Declaration was adopted on July 4, 1776, but wasn't formally signed until August 2, 1776.

100. Name **two** national holidays.

- New Year's Day
- Martin Luther King, Jr. Day
- Presidents' Day
- Memorial Day
- Juneteenth
- Independence Day
- Labor Day
- Columbus Day
- Veterans Day
- Thanksgiving
- Christmas

National holidays are days that Congress has declared to be federal holidays. Generally, most federal employees have these days off work and most government offices are closed. While no one is forced to observe these holidays, all states and most employers observe the majority of them.

Test Yourself

1. What is the supreme law of the land?

2. What does the Constitution do?

3. The idea of self-government is in the first three words of the Constitution. What are these words?

4. What is an amendment?

5. What do we call the first ten amendments to the Constitution?

6. What is <u>one</u> right or freedom from the First Amendment?*

7. How many amendments does the Constitution have?

8. What did the Declaration of Independence do?

9. What are <u>two</u> rights in the Declaration of Independence?

10. What is freedom of religion?

11. What is the economic system in the United States?*

12. What is the "rule of law"?

13. Name <u>one</u> branch or part of the government.*

14. What stops <u>one</u> branch of government from becoming too powerful?

15. Who is in charge of the executive branch?

16. Who makes federal laws?

17. What are the <u>two</u> parts of the U.S. Congress?*

18. How many U.S. Senators are there?

19. We elect a U.S. Senator for how many years?

20. Who is <u>one</u> of your state's U.S. Senators now?*

21. The House of Representatives has how many voting members?

22. We elect a U.S. Representative for how many years?

23. Name your U.S. Representative.

24. Who does a U.S. Senator represent?

25. Why do some states have more Representatives than other states?

26. We elect a President for how many years?

27. In what month do we vote for President?*

28. What is the name of the President of the United States now?*

29. What is the name of the Vice President of the United States now?

30. If the President can no longer serve, who becomes President?

31. If both the President and the Vice President can no longer serve, who becomes President?

32. Who is the Commander in Chief of the military?

33. Who signs bills to become laws?

34. Who vetoes bills?

35. What does the President's Cabinet do?

36. What are <u>two</u> Cabinet-level positions?

37. What does the judicial branch do?

38. What is the highest court in the United States?

39. How many justices are on the Supreme Court?

40. Who is the Chief Justice of the United States now?

41. Under our Constitution, some powers belong to the federal government. What is <u>one</u> power of the federal government?

42. Under our Constitution, some powers belong to the states. What is <u>one</u> power of the states?

43. Who is the Governor of your state now?

44. What is the capital of your state?*

45. What are the two major political parties in the United States?*

46. What is the political party of the President now?

47. What is the name of the Speaker of the House of Representatives now?

48. There are four amendments to the Constitution about who can vote. Describe <u>one</u> of them.

49. What is __one__ responsibility that is only for United States citizens?*

50. Name __one__ right only for United States citizens.

51. What are __two__ rights of everyone living in the United States?

52. What do we show loyalty to when we say the Pledge of Allegiance?

53. What is __one__ promise you make when you become a United States citizen?

54. How old do citizens have to be to vote for President?*

55. What are <u>two</u> ways that Americans can participate in their democracy?

56. When is the last day you can send in federal income tax forms?*

57. When must all men register for the Selective Service?

58. What is <u>one</u> reason colonists came to America?

59. Who lived in America before the Europeans arrived?

60. What group of people was taken to America and sold as slaves?

61. Why did the colonists fight the British?

62. Who wrote the Declaration of Independence?

63. When was the Declaration of Independence adopted?

64. There were 13 original states. Name three.

65. What happened at the Constitutional Convention?

66. When was the Constitution written?

67. The Federalist Papers supported the passage of the U.S. Constitution. Name one of the writers.

68. What is one thing Benjamin Franklin is famous for?

69. Who is the "Father of Our Country"?

70. Who was the first President?*

71. What territory did the United States buy from France in 1803?

72. Name <u>one</u> war fought by the United States in the 1800s.

73. Name the U.S. war between the North and the South.

74. Name <u>one</u> problem that led to the Civil War.

75. What was <u>one</u> important thing that Abraham Lincoln did?*

76. What did the Emancipation Proclamation do?

77. What did Susan B. Anthony do?

78. Name <u>one</u> war fought by the United States in the 1900s. *

79. Who was President during World War I?

80. Who was the President during the Great Depression and World War II?

81. Who did the United States fight in World War II?

82. Before he was President, Eisenhower was a general. What war was he in?

83. During the Cold War, what was the main concern of the United States?

84. What movement tried to end racial discrimination?

85. What did Martin Luther King Jr. do?*

86. What major event happened on September 11, 2001, in the United States?

87. Name one American Indian tribe in the United States.

88. Name one of the two longest rivers in the United States.

89. What ocean is on the West Coast of the United States?

90. What ocean is on the East Coast of the United States?

91. Name <u>one</u> U.S. territory.

92. Name <u>one</u> state that borders Canada.

93. Name <u>one</u> state that borders Mexico.

94. What is the capital of the United States?*

95. Where is the Statue of Liberty?*

96. Why does the flag have 13 stripes?

97. Why does the flag have 50 stars?*

98. What is the name of the national anthem?

99. When do we celebrate Independence Day?*

100. Name <u>two</u> national holidays.

Practice Test #1

9. What are <u>two</u> rights in the Declaration of Independence?

76. What did the Emancipation Proclamation do?

84. What movement tried to end racial discrimination?

46. What is the political party of the President now?

48. There are four amendments to the Constitution about who can vote. Describe <u>one</u> of them.

78. Name <u>one</u> war fought by the United States in the 1900s.*

67. The Federalist Papers supported the passage of the U.S. Constitution. Name <u>one</u> of the writers.

64. There were 13 original states. Name <u>three</u>.

70. Who was the first President?*

38. What is the highest court in the United States?

Answer Explanations #1

9. What are <u>two</u> rights in the Declaration of Independence?

- Life
- Liberty
- Pursuit of happiness

76. What did the Emancipation Proclamation do?

- Freed the slaves
- Freed slaves in the Confederacy
- Freed slaves in the Confederate states
- Freed slaves in most Southern states

84. What movement tried to end racial discrimination?

- Civil Rights Movement

46. What is the political party of the President now?

- Democratic (party)

The answer to this question can change. Access this website for up-to-date information:

testprepbooks.com/civics

48. There are four amendments to the Constitution about who can vote. Describe <u>one</u> of them.

- Citizens eighteen (18) and older (can vote).
- You don't have to pay (a poll tax) to vote.
- Any citizen can vote. (Women and men can vote.)
- A male citizen of any race (can vote).

78. Name <u>one</u> war fought by the United States in the 1900s.*

- World War I
- World War II
- Korean War
- Vietnam War
- (Persian) Gulf War

67. The Federalist Papers supported the passage of the U.S. Constitution. Name <u>one</u> of the writers.

- James Madison
- Alexander Hamilton
- John Jay
- Publius

64. There were 13 original states. Name three.

- New Hampshire
- Massachusetts
- Rhode Island
- Connecticut
- New York
- New Jersey
- Pennsylvania
- Delaware
- Maryland
- Virginia
- North Carolina
- South Carolina
- Georgia

70. Who was the first President?*

- George Washington

38. What is the highest court in the United States?

- The Supreme Court

Practice Test #2

11. What is the economic system in the United States?*

14. What stops <u>one</u> branch of government from becoming too powerful?

43. Who is the Governor of your state now?

56. When is the last day you can send in federal income tax forms?*

90. What ocean is on the East Coast of the United States?

81. Who did the United States fight in World War II?

32. Who is the Commander in Chief of the military?

35. What does the President's Cabinet do?

44. What is the capital of your state?*

12. What is the "rule of law"?

Answer Explanations #2

11. What is the economic system in the United States?*

- Capitalist economy
- Market economy

14. What stops <u>one</u> branch of government from becoming too powerful?

- Checks and balances
- Separation of powers

43. Who is the Governor of your state now?

- Answers will vary

You can find your Governor here:

testprepbooks.com/civics

District of Columbia residents should answer that D.C. does not have a Governor.

56. When is the last day you can send in federal income tax forms?*

- April 15

90. What ocean is on the East Coast of the United States?

- Atlantic Ocean

81. Who did the United States fight in World War II?

- Japan, Germany, and Italy

32. Who is the Commander in Chief of the military?

- The President

35. What does the President's Cabinet do?

- Advises the President

44. What is the capital of your state?*

- Answers will vary.

You can find your state capital here:

testprepbooks.com/civics

District of Columbia residents should answer that D.C. is not a state and does not have a capital. Residents of U.S. territories should name the capital of the territory.

12. What is the "rule of law"?

- Everyone must follow the law.
- Leaders must obey the law.
- Government must obey the law.
- No one is above the law.

Practice Test #3

30. If the President can no longer serve, who becomes President?

55. What are <u>two</u> ways that Americans can participate in their democracy?

16. Who makes federal laws?

26. We elect a President for how many years?

18. How many U.S. Senators are there?

17. What are the <u>two</u> parts of the U.S. Congress?*

91. Name <u>one</u> U.S. territory.

51. What are <u>two</u> rights of everyone living in the United States?

58. What is <u>one</u> reason colonists came to America?

45. What are the <u>two</u> major political parties in the United States?*

Answer Explanations #3

30. If the President can no longer serve, who becomes President?

- The Vice President

55. What are <u>two</u> ways that Americans can participate in their democracy?

- Vote
- Join a political party
- Help with a campaign
- Join a civic group
- Join a community group
- Give an elected official your opinion on an issue
- Call Senators and Representatives
- Publicly support or oppose an issue or policy
- Run for office
- Write to a newspaper

16. Who makes federal laws?

- Congress
- Senate and House of Representatives
- U.S. or national legislature

26. We elect a President for how many years?

- Four (4)

18. How many U.S. Senators are there?

- One hundred (100)

17. What are the <u>two</u> parts of the U.S. Congress?*

- The Senate and the House of Representatives

91. Name <u>one</u> U.S. territory.

- Puerto Rico
- U.S. Virgin Islands
- American Samoa
- Northern Mariana Islands
- Guam

51. What are <u>two</u> rights of everyone living in the United States?

- Freedom of expression
- Freedom of speech
- Freedom of assembly
- Freedom to petition the government
- Freedom of religion
- The right to bear arms

58. What is <u>one</u> reason colonists came to America?

- Freedom
- Political liberty
- Religious freedom
- Economic opportunity
- Practice their religion
- Escape persecution

45. What are the <u>two</u> major political parties in the United States?*

- Democratic and Republican

Practice Test #4

61. Why did the colonists fight the British?

34. Who vetoes bills?

29. What is the name of the Vice President of the United States now?

93. Name <u>one</u> state that borders Mexico.

27. In what month do we vote for President?*

31. If both the President and the Vice President can no longer serve, who becomes President?

15. Who is in charge of the executive branch?

54. How old do citizens have to be to vote for President?*

28. What is the name of the President of the United States now?*

6. What is <u>one</u> right or freedom from the First Amendment?*

Answer Explanations #4

61. Why did the colonists fight the British?

- Because of high taxes (taxation without representation)
- Because the British army stayed in their houses (boarding, quartering)
- Because they didn't have self-government

34. Who vetoes bills?

- The President

29. What is the name of the Vice President of the United States now?

- Kamala D. Harris
- Kamala Harris
- Harris

The answer to this question can change. Access this website for up-to-date information:

testprepbooks.com/civics

93. Name <u>one</u> state that borders Mexico.

- California
- Arizona
- New Mexico
- Texas

27. In what month do we vote for President?*

- November

31. If both the President and the Vice President can no longer serve, who becomes President?

- The Speaker of the House

15. Who is in charge of the executive branch?

- The President

54. How old do citizens have to be to vote for President?*

- Eighteen (18) and older

28. What is the name of the President of the United States now?*

- Joseph R. Biden, Jr.
- Joe Biden
- Biden

The answer to this question can change. Access this website for up-to-date information:

testprepbooks.com/civics

6. What is <u>one</u> right or freedom from the First Amendment?*

- Speech
- Religion
- Assembly
- Press
- Petition the government

Practice Test #5

66. When was the Constitution written?

8. What did the Declaration of Independence do?

60. What group of people was taken to America and sold as slaves?

23. Name your U.S. Representative.

20. Who is <u>one</u> of your state's U.S. Senators now?*

79. Who was President during World War I?

80. Who was the President during the Great Depression and World War II?

72. Name <u>one</u> war fought by the United States in the 1800s.

21. The House of Representatives has how many voting members?

13. Name <u>one</u> branch or part of the government.*

Answer Explanations #5

66. When was the Constitution written?

- 1787

8. What did the Declaration of Independence do?

- Announced our independence from Great Britain
- Declared our independence from Great Britain
- Stated that the United States is free from Great Britain

60. What group of people was taken to America and sold as slaves?

- Africans
- People from Africa

23. Name your U.S. Representative.

- Answers will vary. You can find your U.S. Representative here:

testprepbooks.com/civics

Residents of territories with nonvoting Delegates or Resident Commissioners may provide the name of the Delegate or Commissioner. Also acceptable is any statement that the territory has no (voting) Representatives in Congress.

20. Who is <u>one</u> of your state's U.S. Senators now?*

- Answers will vary according to your state. You can find your U.S. Senators here:

testprepbooks.com/civics

District of Columbia residents and residents of U.S. territories should answer that D.C. (or the territory where the applicant lives) has no U.S. Senators.

79. Who was President during World War I?

- Woodrow Wilson

80. Who was the President during the Great Depression and World War II?

- Franklin Roosevelt

72. Name <u>one</u> war fought by the United States in the 1800s.

- War of 1812
- Mexican-American War
- Civil War
- Spanish-American War

21. The House of Representatives has how many voting members?

- Four hundred thirty-five (435)

13. Name <u>one</u> branch or part of the government.*

- Congress
- Legislative
- President
- Executive
- The courts
- Judicial